Why Why Why

were mammoths woolly?

MC
PUBLISHERS

First published as hardback in 2006 by
Miles Kelly Publishing Ltd, Bardfield Centre,
Great Bardfield, Essex, CM7 4SLCopyright
© Miles Kelly Publishing Ltd 2006

This 2009 edition published and distributed
by:

Mason Crest Publishers Inc.
370 Reed Road, Broomall, Pennsylvania
19008
(866) MCP-BOOK (toll free)
www.masoncrest.com

Why Why Why—
Were Mammoths Woolly?
ISBN 978-1-4222-1589-0
Library of Congress Cataloging-in-
Publication data is available

Why Why Why—?
Complete 23 Title Series
ISBN 978-1-4222-1568-5

Printed in the United States of America

Contents

What was an ammonite?

An ammonite was a sea creature that lived millions of years ago. It had big eyes and long tentacles that it used like arms to catch its prey. The ammonite's soft body was protected by a shell.

Ammonite

Suckers!

The first fish could not bite — they were suckers! They had no jaws or teeth, and probably sucked in worms and bits of food from the mud.

Which fish wore armor?

Cephalaspis (sef-ah-las-pis) was an early type of fish that had a big shield of bony armor around its head. The armor protected the fish from other animals and also helped *Cephalaspis* scoop up mud to find worms to eat. This fish spent most of its time on the seabed searching for food.

Cephalaspis

Were fish bigger than cars?

Dunkleosteus (dunk-lee-owe-stee-us) was! It grew up to 32 feet long – that's as long as a truck! *Dunkleosteus* had huge teeth, made of narrow blades of bone. These could slice through the bones of the fish it ate.

Think

Can you think of any other creatures that have a shell?

Which scorpion was as big as a lion?

The giant sea scorpion *Pterygotus* (terry-got-us) was. It was one of the first hunting animals. *Pterygotus* used its tail to chase prey, which it tore apart with its claws. Unlike today's scorpions, *Pterygotus* had no sting in its tail.

Pterygotus

Why did fish begin to walk?

So they could reach more water when their pools dried up. *Eusthenopteron* (use-then-op-teron) had lungs for breathing air and walked using its fins. It was 3 feet in length and ate other fish.

Eusthenopteron

Which sea creature swam slowly?

Plesiosaurus (ples-ee-oh-sore-us) lived in the sea but was a slow swimmer. Its tail was not very strong, so it used its flipper-like fins to swim, but it could still catch fish and squid to eat.

What was a trilobite?

Trilobite

A trilobite was a sea creature that lived millions of years ago. It moved quickly along the seabed looking for food. A trilobite could roll up into a ball, just like a woodlouse can today. This gave protection, as the hard shell stopped other creatures from attacking it.

Dolphin look-alikes

Ichthyosaurs (ik-thee-oh-sores) were sea reptiles that looked similar to dolphins of today. However ichthyosaurs had simpler brains and were less intelligent than dolphins!

Copy
A trilobite could roll its body into a ball. See how well you can roll into a ball.

Which creature had 32 toes?

Acanthostega, (a-can-tho-stee-ga), the first four-legged animal, had eight toes on each foot. It used its toes to grip water plants as it swam. *Acanthostega* spent most of its time in water, but it could live on land, too.

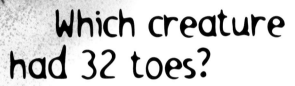

Acanthostega

Did reptiles fly?

Some did! Pterosaurs (terr-oh-sores) were flying reptiles. They had thin, skin-covered wings. Their tails helped them to balance as they flew. Some had fangs in their mouths with small, spiky teeth behind them.

When were millipedes like monsters?

Giant millipede

Millions of years ago, millipedes were like huge monsters, measuring more than 6 feet in length. They were among the first animals to leave the sea and live on land. These creepy-crawlies ate rotting plants and lived in forests.

Measure

Use a tape measure and find out how long giant millipedes were. Are they much bigger than you?

What was the biggest insect?

Meganeura (meg-an-ner-rah) was a giant dragonfly, and it was the biggest insect ever to have lived. From one wing to the other it measured more than 18 inches in length. It attacked and ate other insects. *Meganeura's* large eyes helped it to spot its prey.

Dino-croc!

The first crocodiles lived before the dinosaurs. Crocodiles still exist today, long after the dinosaurs have gone.

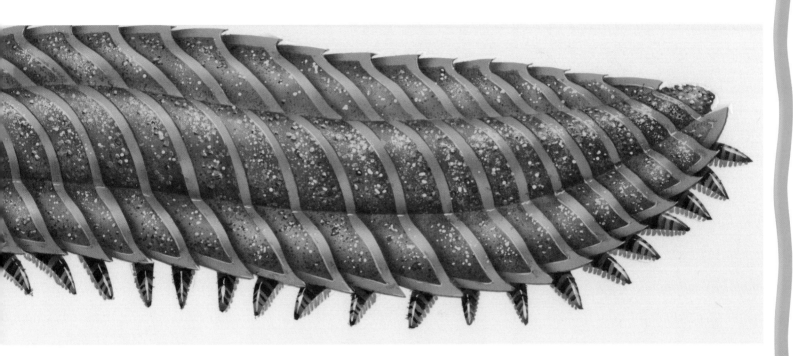

Which reptile hated the rain?

Diictodon (dik-tow-don) used its strong legs and claws to dig holes to shelter from bad weather.

It didn't like to be too hot or cold, and hated getting wet. It had a beak-like mouth and sharp teeth to cut up tough plant food.

Diictodon

Were any reptiles furry?

Most reptiles have scaly skin, but *Cynognathus* (sy-nog-nay-thus) was a furry reptile. It was the size of a large dog and had very strong jaws that could bite through bone. The name *Cynognathus* means 'dog jaw'. It could run very fast to hunt its prey.

Cynognathus

When were horses slow runners?

Hyracotherium (hi-rack-oh-ther-ee-um) was an early type of horse. Its short legs meant it couldn't run very fast.

Terrible teeth!

Mastodonsaurus (mast-o-don-sore-us) had two front teeth that may have poked through its snout. Apart from these teeth, it looked similar to modern crocodiles.

Which creature had chisel-like teeth?

A reptile called *Moschops* did. They were long and straight, with a sharp edge. *Moschops* could easily bite through leaves and twigs on bushes. It was as big as a rhinoceros.

Moschops

Draw
Sketch a picture of *Moschops* eating leaves. Don't forget its sharp teeth.

Which creature had the bendiest neck?

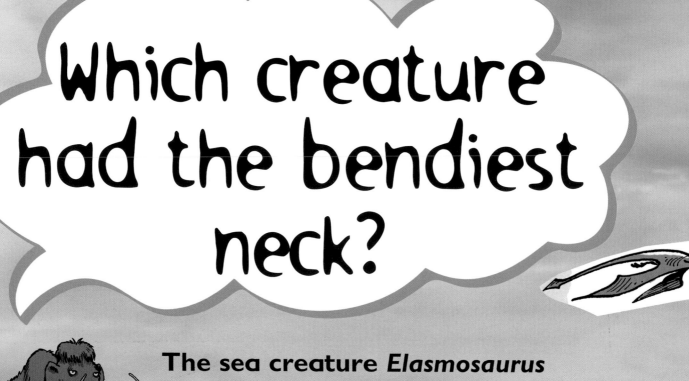

The sea creature _Elasmosaurus_ (el-as-mo-sore-us) did. Its neck measured over 16 feet long. _Elasmosaurus_ could twist its head around in a circle to look for food such as fish and squid.

Pteranodon

Elasmosaurus

What was the largest flying animal ?

Quetzalcoatlus (ket-sal-co-at-lus) was a flying reptile, and the biggest flying animal of all time. Its wings measured 46 feet from tip to tip. It may have eaten like a vulture, pecking at the bodies of dead animals.

Protosuchus

Think

Elasmosaurus had a very bendy neck. Can you think of any other creatures that have long or bendy necks?

Hopping mad!

Scientists think a reptile called *Lagosuchus* (lag-o-sook-us) may have hopped like a rabbit. *Lagosuchus* means 'rabbit crocodile'!

Do all crocodiles like water?

No, the first crocodiles hated water! *Protosuchus* (pro-tow-sook-us) preferred dry land. It looked very similar to modern crocodiles. *Protosuchus* had long legs to help it run on land, and powerful jaws to snap at prey.

Where did the first whales live?

On dry land! The first whales had legs instead of flippers and hunted other animals. Gradually, they began to spend more time in water and their legs became more flipper-like. *Pakicetus* (pak-ee-set-us) was an early whale that lived both on land and in water.

Pakicetus

Which reptile had a sail?

Dimetrodon (di-metro-don) had a large fin on its back that looked like a sail. The sail helped *Dimetrodon's* body to warm up quickly by absorbing heat from the Sun. If it needed to cool down, *Dimetrodon* stood in the shade.

Discover
Dimetrodon could warm up very quickly. Rub your hands together fast, do they feel warmer?

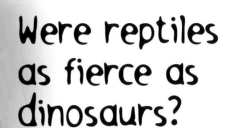
Were reptiles as fierce as dinosaurs?

Mosasaurus (mos-ah-sore-us) was! It was a huge sea reptile with razor-sharp teeth. Weighing up to 10 tons and growing around 33 feet in length — it was far bigger than today's great white shark. *Mosasaurus* was speedy for its size, and swam fast to catch its prey.

Mosasaurus

What was a thunder beast?

Brontotherium (bron-tow-ther-i-um) looked like a huge rhino, and its name means 'thunder beast'. The males used their Y-shaped horns to fight one another to become leaders of the herd. *Brontotherium* was about the size of a rhino.

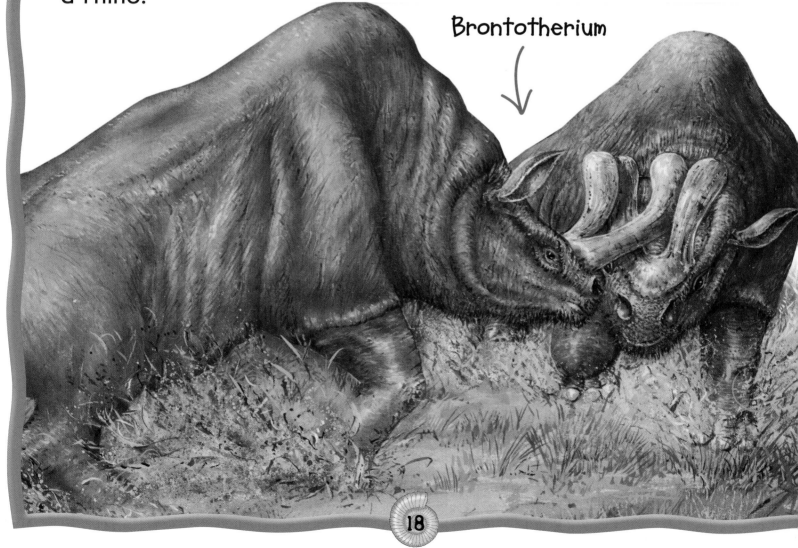

Brontotherium

Have elephants always had trunks?

Early elephants didn't have trunks — they had snouts instead. *Moeritherium* (mee-ri-ther-i-rum), was an early type of elephant. It looked like a pig with a long snout. Over time, elephant trunks have become longer.

Andrewsarchus

Which creature was a big-head?

Andrewsarchus (an-drew-sar-cus) had the biggest head of any hunting land animal. Its head was 3 feet in length, and its teeth were capable of crushing bone.

Make

Using cardboard tubes and sticky tape, see if you can make an elephant trunk. Attach some string so you can wear it!

What animals lived in the Ice Age?

Animals such as woolly mammoths, woolly rhinos and caves lions did. They had thick fur coats that kept them warm. Woolly mammoths and rhinos had long tusks and horns and ate plants. Cave lions were fierce meat eaters with long, sharp teeth.

Count

How many different types of mammal can you count in this picture?

Woolly rhinoceros

Cave lion

Terrific tusks!

The tusks of Anancus (a-nan-cus), a type of early elephant, were over 13 feet in length – almost as long as the animal itself.

Can mammoths freeze?

Yes they can! The bodies of mammoths have been found frozen in ice in cold places such as Russia. The ice stopped the bodies from rotting away, and sometimes the mammoths' fur can still be seen.

Why were mammoths woolly?

To keep them warm! Thick, long hairy coats helped keep out the cold. A deep layer of fat under their skin meant their body heat was kept in. Woolly mammoths could grow up to 10 feet in height and weigh 3 tons.

Aurochs

Megaloceros

Woolly mammoth

Which mammoth wasn't woolly?

The Columbian mammoth wasn't. It lived in North America where the weather was hotter, so it didn't need a woolly coat. Mammoths used their long tusks to defend themselves against attackers.

Think
Today, all horses have hooves instead of toes. Can you think of any other animals that have hooves?

Have horses always had hooves?

No, they used to have toes instead. The first horses had five toes on each foot. Over time, the toes joined together to become hooves. An early horse, *Hyracotherium*, was about the same size as a fox.

Hyracotherium

Columbian mammoth

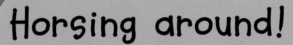

Horsing around!

Thousands of years ago, horses died out in the Americas. Spanish travellers reintroduced horses to this area about 500 years ago.

Which lions began life as dogs?

Sea lions did! The bones of *Allodesmus* (ah-low-des-mus), an early sea lion, show it was closely related to early types of dog. *Allodesmus* had strong flippers that meant it could swim fast.

What was a sabre tooth?

Smilodon

A sabre tooth was a type of cat. Its teeth were long and sharp like knives to stab at prey. *Smilodon* (smi-low-don) attacked slow moving animals such as mammoths.

Jump
Procoptoden could jump along quickly. Have a jumping race with your friends — who can jump the fastest?

Shovel-tusker!

An early elephant called *Platybelodon* (plat-ee-bell-oh-don), is known as 'shovel-tusker'. Scientists think it used the tusks at the end of its trunk to shovel plants into its mouth.

Which dog ate plants?

Hesperocyon, an early type of dog, would eat plants when prey was scarce. *Hesperocyon* was only the size of a pet cat. The first dogs hunted in packs, which helped them to catch much larger animals than if they hunted on their own.

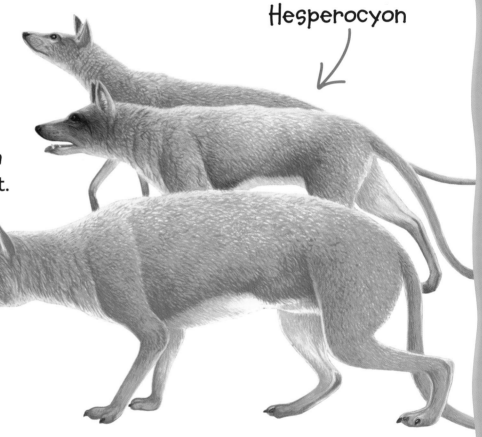

Hesperocyon

Do giant kangaroos exist?

Not today, but they did! *Procoptoden* (pro-cop-tow-don), an early type of kangaroo, was twice as big as modern kangaroos. It grew up to 10 feet in height – that's taller than a door. *Procoptoden* could jump along as fast as a race horse can run – around 40 miles per hour.

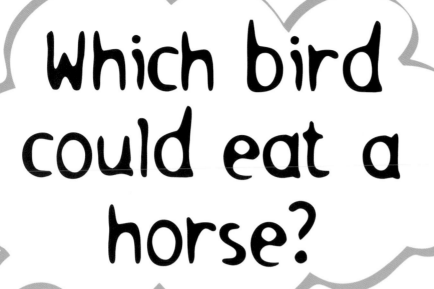

Which bird could eat a horse?

Titanis (tie-tan-is) was a huge hunting bird that ate horses. It lived in South America and grew up to 10 feet in height – far bigger than the first horses. *Titanis* chased after its prey, and tore it apart with its hooked beak.

Titanis

Early horse

Argentavis

Find
Argentavis had very long feathers. What is the longest feather you can find?

Which bird was as big as a plane?

Argentavis (ah-jen-tav-is) was the size of a small plane. Its wings measured 20 feet from tip to tip. It was a kind of vulture that fed on dead animals. The feathers of *Argentavis* measured up to 5 feet in length.

The early bird!
The first flying birds lived at the time of the dinosaurs. However, many of the birds that appeared after the dinosaurs died out, could not fly at all!

Could birds run fast?

Gastornis (gas-torn-is) could. It had long, powerful legs. *Gastornis* could not fly as it was too big and heavy, so it needed to be able to chase after its prey. It may also have hidden in thick forests then leapt out to attack animals as they passed by.

Which animal was as big as a tank?

Glyptodon (glip-tow-don) was a giant armadillo the size of a tank. It was covered in thick, bony armor. *Glyptodon* was over 12 feet in length. It had a bony-studded tail that it used to protect itself from predators.

Boomerang!

A creature called *Diplocaulus* (dip-low-call-us) had a boomerang-shaped head. This may have stopped attackers from swallowing *Diplocaulus*!

Which sloth was as big as a tree?

Megatherium (mega-ther-i-um) was a giant sloth that grew up to 20 feet tall — that's the same height as some trees. However it was far too heavy to climb trees as it weighed up to 3 tons.

Megatherium

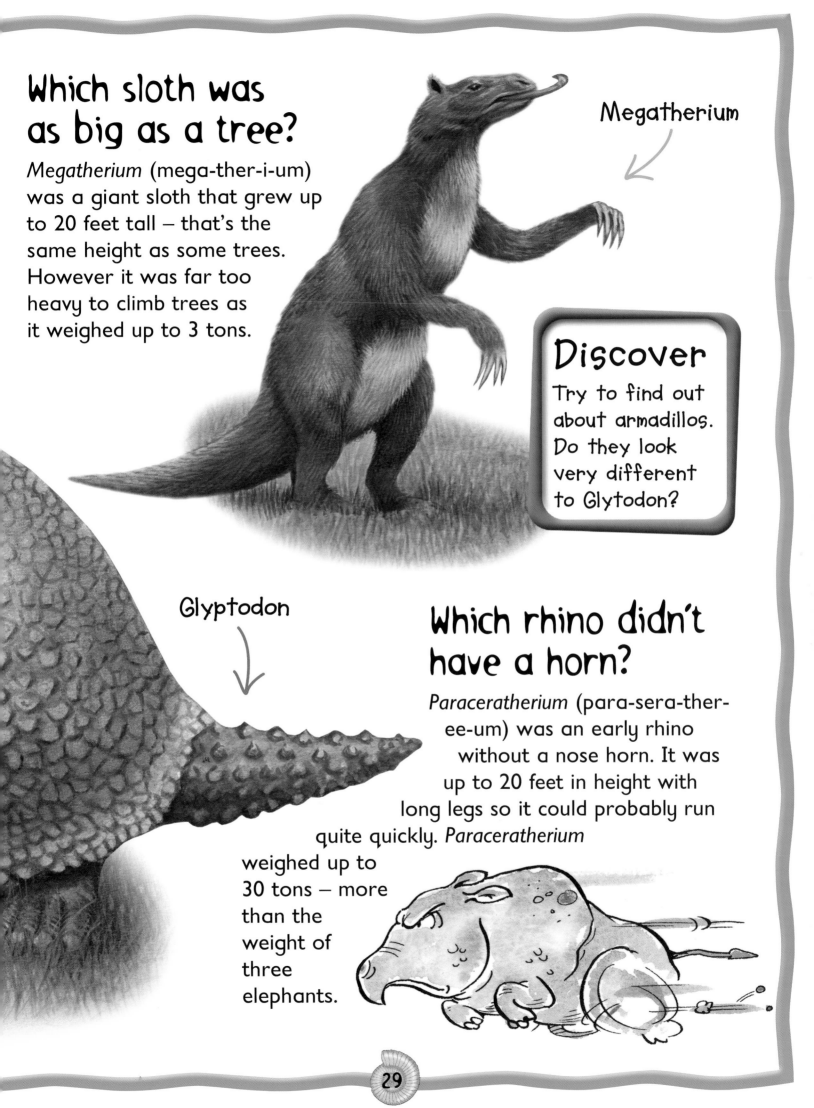

Discover

Try to find out about armadillos. Do they look very different to Glytodon?

Glyptodon

Which rhino didn't have a horn?

Paraceratherium (para-sera-ther-ee-um) was an early rhino without a nose horn. It was up to 20 feet in height with long legs so it could probably run quite quickly. *Paraceratherium* weighed up to 30 tons — more than the weight of three elephants.

29

Quiz time

page 10

Do you remember what you have read about prehistoric animals? These questions will test your memory. The pictures will help you. If you get stuck, read the pages again.

4. What was the biggest insect?

page 12

5. Were any reptiles furry ?

page 5

1. Were any fish bigger than cars?

page 15

6. What was the largest flying animal?

2. Which scorpion was as big as a lion?

page 6

7. Were reptiles as fierce as dinosaurs?

page 9

3. Did reptiles fly?

page 17

8. Have elephants always had trunks?

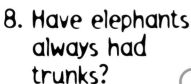

page 19

12. Which bird was as big as a small plane?

page 27

9. Can mammoths freeze?

page 21

page 29

13. Which rhino didn't have a horn?

10. Have horses always had hooves?

page 23

11. Do giant kangaroos exist today?

page 25

Answers

1. Yes, some were
2. Pterygotus
3. Yes, some could
4. Meganeura
5. Yes, some were
6. Quetzalcoatlus
7. Yes, some were
8. No, early elephants had snouts
9. Yes they can!
10. No, they used to have toes
11. Not today, but they once did!
12. Argentavis
13. Paraceratherium

Index